DATE DUE

Music
HALL OF FAME

Morgan Hughes

The Rourke Book Company, Inc.
Vero Beach, Florida 32964

PHOTO CREDITS:
Cover, pages 4-7 courtesy of the Rock and Roll Hall of Fame, Cleveland, OH; pages 9-13, 16-22 ©
Archive Photos, New York, NY; page 15 courtesy of the Gospel Hall of Fame, Detroit, MI

PRODUCED & DESIGNED by East Coast Studios
eastcoaststudios.com

EDITORIAL SERVICES:
Janice L. Smith for Penworthy Learning Systems
Pamela Schroeder

Library of Congress Cataloging-in-Publication Data

Hughes, Morgan, 1957-
    Music / Morgan E. Hughes.
        p. cm. — (Halls of fame)
    Includes index.
    Summary: Describes seven Halls of Fame that honor special people and
accomplishments in music, including the Rock 'n' Roll Hall of Fame, the International
Harmonica Hall of Fame, and the American Classical Music Hall of Fame.
    ISBN 1-55916-269-4
    1. Music museums—United States—Directories—Juvenile literature. 2. Halls of fame—United States—
Directories—Juvenile literature. [1. Music museums. 2. Halls of fame. 3. Museums.] I. Title.

ML13 .H84 2000
780'.74'73—dc21

                                                                    00–023698

Printed in the USA

Table of Contents

Rock and Roll Hall of Fame

Every man, woman, girl, and boy in America loves some kind of music. It might be classical or country music, jazz or bluegrass. The choices are endless. Music is the "common" language of the world, a language everyone speaks.

The Rock and Roll Hall of Fame in Cleveland, Ohio, honors the men and women who created rock 'n' roll. Rock 'n' roll is one of the most popular kinds of music in the world.

Elvis Presley's life and music are celebrated at the Rock and Roll Hall of Fame.

Rock 'n' roll includes parts of other types of music. Such legends as Hank Williams, Johnny Cash, Jerry Lee Lewis, and Carl Perkins brought a piece of country music to rock 'n' roll. Others, like Aretha Franklin, The Supremes, Gladys Knight & The Pips, and Stevie Wonder added gospel sounds as well as the **distinctive** (dis TINGK tiv) sound of rhythm and blues.

At the Hall of Fame, you can see Woody Guthrie's mandolin and John Lennon's 1964 Rickenbacker guitar.

Visitors to the Rock and Roll Hall of Fame need plenty of time to see the 150,000 square feet of displays.

Later, the British gave rock 'n' roll a new sound, thanks to The Beatles, The Rolling Stones, Eric Clapton, David Bowie, Elton John, and many more.

Located at One Key Plaza in Cleveland, the Rock and Roll Hall of Fame is open year-round. You can find its website at *www.rockhall.com*.

Country Music Hall of Fame

The Country Music Hall of Fame is located in Nashville, Tennessee. This southern city is the "home" of country music. The Hall of Fame lets you take a great journey through the history of America's heartland music.

You can learn all about the king and queen of country music, Hank Williams and Patsy Cline. Williams and Cline, huge stars in the 1950s, helped to shape the future of country music.

Hank Williams is the grandfather of country western music.

THEATRE
PRESENTS
in PERSON
PATSY
CLINE
TOMPALL
GLAZIER BROS.

The Hall of Fame has the guitar Garth Brooks smashed during one concert. You can also find the water skis Allan Jackson used when he made the music video for his song "Chattahoochee." A 20-foot-long (6-meter-long) guitar Travis Tritt used in one of his videos is also there.

At the Country Music Hall of Fame, you can watch **vintage** (VINT ij) film clips. You can also look at items that belonged to hundreds of country music stars.

For more information, call 800-816-7652 or visit the website *www.coww.com/cow/cmhf*.

Patsy Cline won over millions of fans with her version of the song, "San Antonio Rose."

International Harmonica Hall of Fame

The International Harmonica Hall of Fame is not located in a building. It is a **cyberspace** (SIE ber SPAYS) Hall of Fame. It is dedicated to making sure that the art of harmonica playing never dies. Harmonica music is an important style from early America. You may be a professional player or you may play just for the love of it. Either way, the International Harmonica Hall of Fame hopes you never stop.

In the early 1960s, Bob Dylan added the harmonica to rock music.

Stevie Wonder's great rhythm and blues sound was made even better by his "harp" playing.

At your computer you can read about the lives of harmonica players from yesterday to today. This growing Hall of Fame welcomes stories, pictures, old posters, or news about harmonica playing and players.

You can visit the International Harmonica Hall of Fame at *www.montanastore.com/ mtstore/ihhf/index.htm.*

Gospel Music Hall of Fame

Gospel music is a music that began only in America. It can be traced back to the terrible times of slavery. Gospel music has always been a very **spiritual** (SPIR ich oo ul) and hopeful kind of music. Many of the songs are about faith and finding the strength to live through **adversity** (ad VER sut ee).

The Gospel Music Hall of Fame and Museum is located in Detroit, Michigan (also known as Motown). It was started in 1995 by recording artist David Gough. He is known as the Mayor of Gospel.

For more information on the Gospel Music Hall of Fame, call 313-592-0017 or visit its website at *www.gmfh.org*.

David Gough's Gospel Hall of Fame honors those who sing or play this "hand-clapping, soul-stirring, heartfelt" music.

Reggae Hall of Fame

The Reggae Hall of Fame, a cyberspace shrine, was created by Toney Campbell. Campbell worked in radio and television and he loves **reggae** (REG ay) music. The Reggae Hall of Fame honors the artists who have made this music so popular. Also, it helps people learn about reggae **culture** (KUL chur).

The legends of reggae music include Bob Marley & The Wailers, Jimmy Cliff, Burning Star, and Sly & Robbie. From the roots of reggae, new styles like ska, dancehall, and dub music have been born.

You can learn more by visiting the Reggae Hall of Fame website at *www.reggaehalloffame.com* or by calling 281-859-2234.

Before his death, Bob Marley was reggae's most popular and well-known performer.

American Classical Music Hall of Fame

Classical music is one of the most highly-respected kinds of music anywhere in the world. You may hear this type of music in an opera or a ballet, or at an orchestra or symphony **recital** (ri SIT ul).

A classical music genius, Ludwig van Beethoven wrote music even after he went deaf.

Luciano Pavarotti is the most famous and (many say) gifted tenor of the late 20th century.

The American Classical Music Hall of Fame honors the men and women who have given their talent to this kind of music.

The American Classical Music Hall of Fame and Museum is located in Cleveland, Ohio. You can find out more at the website *www.ClassicalHall.org*.

Rockabilly Hall of Fame

You might tell from its name that rockabilly mixes rock 'n' roll and country (or hillbilly) music. In the 1950s, guitar player Carl Perkins was one of the first rockabilly artists. In the 1980s, Englishman Dave Edmunds became a star of this type of music.

At the cyberspace Rockabilly Hall of Fame, you can read about more than 100 men and women who have played rockabilly music since the mid-1900s.

If you have questions or would like to add to the Rockabilly Hall of Fame, visit its website at *www.dataex.com/~genevinc.*

After the rock 'n' roll British invasion, England's Dave Edmunds became a rockabilly star.

GLOSSARY

adversity (ad VER sut ee) — bad fortune, misfortune, no luck

culture (KUL chur) — what people make and think about during a time period in history

cyberspace (SIE ber SPAYS) — a modern way of saying "on the internet"

distinctive (dis TINGK tiv) — something that sets a person or group apart from others

recital (ri SIT ul) — a concert; public display of skill

reggae (REG ay) — a popular music from Jamaica that mixes soul music and rock 'n' roll

spiritual (SPIR ich oo ul) — having to do with a church or religion

vintage (VINT ij) — a style that was popular in the past

Carl Perkins was a guitar player whose style and talent made him the king of rockabilly music.

INDEX